The Big Balloon Race

story by Eleanor Coerr
pictures by Carolyn Croll

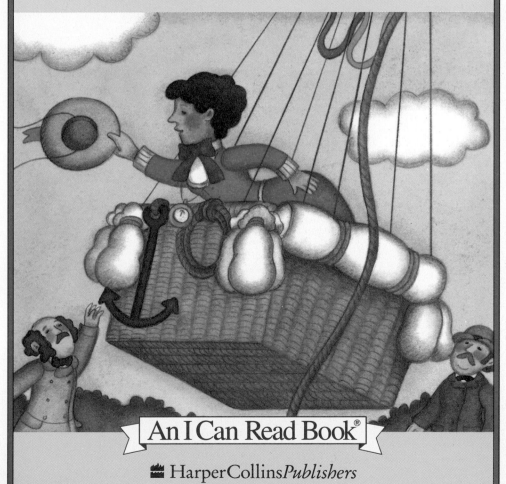

An I Can Read Book®

HarperCollinsPublishers

For Julian, balloon detective
—E.C.

For Joshua and Anna
—C.C.

This book is a presentation of Newfield Publications, Inc.
Newfield Publications offers book clubs for children
from preschool through high school. For further
information write to: **Newfield Publications, Inc.**,
4343 Equity Drive, Columbus, Ohio 43228.

Published by arrangement with HarperCollins Publishers.
Newfield Publications is a trademark
of Newfield Publications, Inc.
I Can Read Book is a
registered trademark of HarperCollins Publishers.

THE BIG BALLOON RACE
Text copyright © 1981 by Eleanor Coerr
Illustrations copyright © 1981, 1992 by Carolyn Croll
Printed in the U.S.A. All rights reserved.
1 2 3 4 5 6 7 8 9 10
Newly Illustrated Edition

Library of Congress Cataloging-in-Publication Data

Coerr, Eleanor
The big balloon race
by Eleanor Coerr; illustrations by Carolyn Croll.
p. cm. – (An I can read book)
Originally published: New York, N.Y. :
Harper & Row, © 1981.
Summary: Ariel almost causes her famous mother
to lose a balloon race and then helps her win it.
ISBN 0-06-021352-3. – ISBN 0-06-021353-1 (lib. bdg.)
1. Myers, Carlotta, 1849-1932 – Juvenile fiction.
2. Myers, Ariel – Juvenile fiction.
[1. Myers, Carlotta, 1849-1932 – Fiction.
2. Myers, Ariel – Fiction.
3. Balloon ascensions – Fiction.]
I. Croll, Carolyn, ill. II. Title. III. Series
[PZ7.C6567Bi 1992]   91-13606
[E] – dc20   CIP   AC

~ Contents ~

~ 1 ~

Balloons, Balloons!

It was the day

of the big balloon race.

Ariel got up early

and hurried to her mother's room.

"Please," she asked, "can I go up

in the balloon with you?"

Carlotta the Great

was putting on her blue dress

with the fancy gold braid.

"You are too young," she said,

"and winning a race

is hard work."

"But I can help," said Ariel.

Carlotta smiled.

"You can help by riding

in the buggy with your father

to the finish line."

"Oh, thumps!" said Ariel.

Sadly, she went outside.

Balloon Farm was a strange farm.

In the yard

half-filled balloons sat

like giant mushrooms.

People came from all over

to buy balloons

made by Mr. Myers.

Ariel watched her father

fold Carlotta's balloon, *Lucky Star*.

"I wish I could be an aeronaut

like Mama," she said.

"When you are older,"

said Mr. Myers.

"Now it is time to go."

Carlotta, Ariel, and Mr. Myers

climbed into the buggy.

Lucky Star followed in a wagon.

There was a great whoop-de-doo
at the fairgrounds.
Thousands of people were there
to see the balloon race.
It was a big event in 1882.
OOMPAH! OOMPAH! OOMPAH!
played the band.
Two balloons were already
in the air.
They were tied to the ground
by long ropes.
Acrobats swung from one basket
to the other.

Lucky Star and its net

were spread out on the ground.

PFFFTTTTTT!

Lighter-than-air hydrogen gas

hissed into the balloon.

It slowly grew

until it was taller

than the house

on Balloon Farm.

Twelve strong men

held *Lucky Star* down.

15

Nearby, another balloon

grew fat and tall.

It was *Flying Cloud*,

a ball of bright colors.

Its captain, Bernard the Brave,

was the best gentleman aeronaut

in America.

Carlotta the Great

was the best lady aeronaut.

It would be a close race.

"I bet you will win,"

Ariel told her mother.

Carlotta gave her a kiss.

"You can sit in the basket

until it is time to go."

Ariel got inside the basket

and talked to Harry the pigeon.

Harry went on every flight.

Sometimes he took messages

from Carlotta to Balloon Farm.

The mayor began a long speech.

He talked on and on.

So Ariel climbed inside

the Odds and Ends box.

It was quieter there,

and cozy and warm.

Soon she was fast asleep.

Ariel did not hear

the mayor's last words.

"There is a south wind," he said,

"so the finish line will be

the other side

of Devil's Punchbowl Lake."

Ariel did not even hear the drums.

TARUUUUUM!

The aeronauts

stepped into their baskets.

The crowd cheered.

Mr. Myers waved to Carlotta.

"Good luck!"

She waved her nobby sailor hat.

"Hands off!" Carlotta ordered.

The men let go of the ropes.

With a jolt,

Lucky Star took off.

~ 2 ~
Ups and Downs

Ariel woke up.

"What happened?" she asked.

Carlotta stared.

"Ariel! What have you done?"

she cried.

"We are aloft!"

Ariel looked over the side.

Sure enough,

they were off the ground.

Below, someone yelled, "Stop!

There is a stowaway in that basket!"

Mr. Myers waved his arms

and shouted something.

Ariel waved back.

"Oooo!" she cried.

"It's like being a bird."

She watched the crowd

set out for the finish line.

Some were in buggies,

some were in wagons,

and others were on fast horses.

A crosswind tugged at the balloon.

WHOOOOSH!

Lucky Star swooped away over a farm.

Dogs barked

and ran around in circles.

Pigs squealed.

Chickens squawked.

A horse reared and galloped away.

SCRUUUUNCH!

Lucky Star's basket

scraped the treetops.

"Can we go higher?" asked Ariel.

"The balloon and ballast

are for only one passenger,"

said Carlotta.

"You are extra weight."

She dropped one bag of sand

over the side.

Up went *Lucky Star*.

The farm got smaller and smaller.

It looked like a toy.

Then it was gone.

31

"Dear me!" said Carlotta.

"An updraft is sucking us

into that raincloud."

She pulled on the blue valve rope

to let out some gas.

Lucky Star did not fall.

Ariel stared up into netting

that looked like a spiderweb.

"Why don't you pull

the red rope, too?" she asked.

"That is the rip cord,"

said her mother. "It lets

the gas out all at once."

Carlotta tied her hat snugly

under her chin.

"Sit down!" she ordered.

"And hang on!"

Ariel hugged

her mother's sturdy legs

in their fancy blue gaiters.

Lucky Star was in the middle

of a misty, wet, bumpy cloud.

The basket went back and forth,

up and down,

then around and around.

"I feel sick," said Ariel.

"A good aeronaut keeps calm,"

said Carlotta.

"The balloon will cool

and we will go down."

She was right.

In a few minutes *Lucky Star*

was sailing away from the cloud.

Carlotta checked everything.

"Ropes and toggles

are in fine trim,"

she said.

She read the altimeter

that hung around her neck.

"We are about 2000 feet up."

She studied the map and compass.

"We are heading south."

"Look!" said Ariel.

"The lake is straight ahead."

Just then they saw *Flying Cloud*.

"He is beating us," said Ariel.

"He will win the gold medal."

Carlotta shook her head.

"I have a few tricks yet," she said.

"Perhaps we can find

a faster stream of air below us."

41

She valved out gas.

Down…down…down

went *Lucky Star*.

It was sinking too fast—

and toward a town!

Carlotta tossed handfuls

of sand over the side.

Lucky Star moved up

and skimmed the rooftops.

People stopped whatever

they were doing and stared

at the balloon.

Suddenly wind stung Ariel's cheeks.

"Heigh-ho!" cried Carlotta.

"We found the airstream!"

It was Ariel who first saw

a spiky church steeple

coming toward them.

"Look out!" she yelled.

She closed her eyes and hung on.

Carlotta threw out more sand.

Just in time!

Lucky Star soared over the steeple.

Now *Flying Cloud* was behind.

"If we don't hit another updraft,"

said Carlotta,

"we might win."

Soon they were sweeping

over the lake.

"There is only a little sand left,"

Carlotta said.

"Let's hope the wind

blows us right across."

The air was cold.

Lucky Star's gas cooled.

They went down.

Carlotta tossed out

the last handful of sand.

But it was not enough.

"Oh, thumps!" cried Ariel.

"We'll crash into the lake!"

"Let's keep our wits about us,"

said Carlotta,

"and make the basket lighter."

Ariel helped throw out

a raincoat, rubber boots,

the Odds and Ends box,

and the anchor.

Everything went over the side

except Harry and his cage.

~ 3 ~

Ariel to the Rescue

Lucky Star wobbled

and took a giant step.

"Lean on this side," said Carlotta.

The basket creaked

and tilted toward shore.

Lucky Star was almost there, when

SPLAAAAASH!

The basket plunked into the water.

But it didn't sink.

The balloon kept it afloat.

"We lost the race," cried Ariel,

"and it is all my fault.

I am extra weight."

Ariel knew what she had to do.

She held her nose

and jumped into the lake.

The water was only up to her waist.

"Good gracious!"

said her mother.

"That was brave,

but it will not help.

Even without you,

the basket is too wet and heavy

to go up again."

53

Just then *Flying Cloud*

began to come down.

"Our last chance!" cried Carlotta.

She threw the guide rope to Ariel.

"Pull!

Pull us to shore!

Hurry!"

Ariel grabbed the rope

and waded onto the beach.

Lucky Star was easy to pull

with a balloon holding it up.

"Splendid!" cried Carlotta.

She jumped out and dragged

the basket to higher ground.

A minute later

Flying Cloud landed.

"We won! We won!"

shouted Ariel and Carlotta.

They were laughing and hugging

and crying all at the same time.

Bernard the Brave

anchored his balloon to a tree.

Then he came over

and shook Carlotta's hand.

"Congratulations!" he said.

"I see that *Lucky Star* has a crew."

He wrapped Ariel in a blanket.

"Thank you, sir," said Ariel.

Bernard smiled.

"Why, it is my pleasure."

Carlotta sent Harry home

with a victory message

to Balloon Farm.

Soon the crowd arrived.

Mr. Myers rode up in the buggy.

Carlotta told him

how Ariel had helped win the race.

"Ariel," he said,

"I'm proud of you."

The mayor gave Ariel

the gold medal.

Carlotta hugged Ariel.

"I'm proud of you, too," she said.

"Perhaps you *are* old enough to fly."

Ariel smiled happily.

She was sure of it.

~ Author's Note ~

This book is based on stories about the famous Myers family. Professor Carl Myers was an inventor and balloon maker. On Balloon Farm in Mohawk Valley, New York, he made balloons for his wife, the fearless and beautiful aeronaut Carlotta. She was the most expert and popular balloonist in America during the 1880's. Carlotta made more ascensions in hydrogen balloons than any other aeronaut of her time. She lived from 1849 to 1932.

Her daughter, Ariel, became a balloonist, too. She rode a "Sky Cycle" invented by her father. Ariel pedaled a dirigible inside huge tents and auditoriums across the country.